Francis Frith's
Middlesex

Photographic Memories

Francis Frith's
Middlesex

John Bainbridge

First published in the United Kingdom in 2001 by
Frith Book Company Ltd

Hardback Edition 2001
ISBN 1-85937-158-2

British Library Cataloguing in Publication Data

Francis Frith's Middlesex
John Bainbridge

Frith Book Company Ltd
Frith's Barn, Teffont,
Salisbury, Wiltshire SP3 5QP
Tel: +44 (0) 1722 716 376
Email: info@frithbook.co.uk
www.frithbook.co.uk

Printed and bound in Great Britain

Front Cover: Staines, High Street 1907 57995

AS WITH ANY HISTORICAL DATABASE THE FRITH ARCHIVE IS CONSTANTLY BEING CORRECTED AND IMPROVED
AND THE PUBLISHERS WOULD WELCOME INFORMATION ON OMISSIONS OR INACCURACIES

Contents

Francis Frith: *Victorian Pioneer*

FRANCIS FRITH, Victorian founder of the world-famous photographic archive, was a complex and multi-talented man. A devout Quaker and a highly successful Victorian businessman, he was both philosophic by nature and pioneering in outlook.

By 1855 Francis Frith had already established a wholesale grocery business in Liverpool, and sold it for the astonishing sum of £200,000, which is the equivalent today of over £15,000,000. Now a multi-millionaire, he was able to indulge his passion for travel. As a child he had pored over travel books written by early explorers, and his fancy and imagination had been stirred by family holidays to the sublime mountain regions of Wales and Scotland. 'What a land of spirit-stirring and enriching scenes and places!' he had written. He was to return to these scenes of grandeur in later years to 'recapture the thousands of vivid and tender memories', but with a different purpose. Now in his thirties, and captivated by the new science of photography, Frith set out on a series of pioneering journeys to the Nile regions that occupied him from 1856 until 1860.

Intrigue and Adventure

He took with him on his travels a specially-designed wicker carriage that acted as both dark-room and sleeping chamber. These far-flung journeys were packed with intrigue and adventure. In his life story, written when he was sixty-three, Frith tells of being held captive by bandits, and of fighting 'an awful midnight battle to the very point of surrender with a deadly pack of hungry, wild dogs'. Sporting flowing Arab costume, Frith arrived at Akaba by camel seventy years before Lawrence, where he encountered 'desert princes and rival sheikhs, blazing with jewel-hilted swords'.

During these extraordinary adventures he was assiduously exploring the desert regions bordering the Nile and patiently recording the antiquities and peoples with his camera. He was the first photographer to venture beyond the sixth cataract. Africa was still the mysterious 'Dark Continent', and Stanley and Livingstone's historic meeting was a decade into the future. The conditions for picture taking confound belief. He laboured for hours in his wicker dark-room in the sweltering heat of the desert, while the volatile chemicals fizzed dangerously in their trays. Often he was forced to work in remote tombs and caves where conditions were cooler. Back in London he exhibited his photographs and was 'rapturously cheered' by members of the Royal Society. His reputation as a photographer was made overnight. An eminent modern historian has likened their impact on the population of the time to that on our own generation of the first photographs taken on the surface of the moon.

Venture of a Life-Time

Characteristically, Frith quickly spotted the opportunity to create a new business as a specialist publisher of photographs. He lived in an era of immense and sometimes violent change. For the poor in the early part of Victoria's reign work was a drudge and the hours long, and people had precious little free time to enjoy themselves. Most had no transport other than a cart or gig at their disposal, and had not travelled far beyond the boundaries of their own town or village. However,

by the 1870s, the railways had threaded their way across the country, and Bank Holidays and half-day Saturdays had been made obligatory by Act of Parliament. All of a sudden the ordinary working man and his family were able to enjoy days out and see a little more of the world.

With characteristic business acumen, Francis Frith foresaw that these new tourists would enjoy having souvenirs to commemorate their days out. In 1860 he married Mary Ann Rosling and set out with the intention of photographing every city, town and village in Britain. For the next thirty years he travelled the country by train and by pony and trap, producing fine photographs of seaside resorts and beauty spots that were keenly bought by millions of Victorians. These prints were painstakingly pasted into family albums and pored over during the dark nights of winter, rekindling precious memories of summer excursions.

The Rise of Frith & Co

Frith's studio was soon supplying retail shops all over the country. To meet the demand he gathered about him a small team of photographers, and published the work of independent artist-photographers of the calibre of Roger Fenton and Francis Bedford. In order to gain some understanding of the scale of Frith's business one only has to look at the catalogue issued by Frith & Co in 1886: it runs to some 670 pages, listing not only many thousands of views of the British Isles but also many photographs of most European countries, and China, Japan, the USA and Canada — note the sample page shown above from the hand-written *Frith & Co* ledgers detailing pictures taken. By 1890 Frith had created the greatest specialist photographic publishing company in the world,

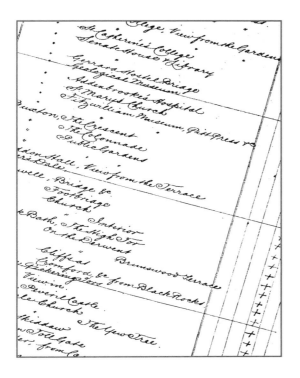

Frith's death, a new card measuring 5.5 x 3.5 inches became the standard format, but it was not until 1902 that the divided back came into being, with address and message on one face and a full-size illustration on the other. *Frith & Co* were in the vanguard of postcard development, and Frith's sons Eustace and Cyril continued their father's monumental task, expanding the number of views offered to the public and recording more and more places in Britain, as the coasts and countryside were opened up to mass travel.

Francis Frith died in 1898 at his villa in Cannes, his great project still growing. The archive he created continued in business for another seventy years. By 1970 it contained over a third of a million pictures of 7,000 cities, towns and villages. The massive photographic record Frith has left to us stands as a living monument to a special and very remarkable man.

with over 2,000 outlets – more than the combined number that Boots and WH Smith have today! The picture on the right shows the *Frith & Co* display board at Ingleton in the Yorkshire Dales. Beautifully constructed with mahogany frame and gilt inserts, it could display up to a dozen local scenes.

Postcard Bonanza

The ever-popular holiday postcard we know today took many years to develop. In 1870 the Post Office issued the first plain cards, with a pre-printed stamp on one face. In 1894 they allowed other publishers' cards to be sent through the mail with an attached adhesive halfpenny stamp. Demand grew rapidly, and in 1895 a new size of postcard was permitted called the court card, but there was little room for illustration. In 1899, a year after

Frith's Archive: *A Unique Legacy*

FRANCIS FRITH'S legacy to us today is of immense significance and value, for the magnificent archive of evocative photographs he created provides a unique record of change in 7,000 cities, towns and villages throughout Britain over a century and more. Frith and his fellow studio photographers revisited locations many times down the years to update their views, compiling for us an enthralling and colourful pageant of British life and character.

We tend to think of Frith's sepia views of Britain as nostalgic, for most of us use them to conjure up memories of places in our own lives with which we have family associations. It often makes us forget that to Francis Frith they were records of daily life as it was actually being lived in the cities, towns and villages of his day. The Victorian age was one of great and often bewildering change for ordinary people, and though the pictures evoke an impression of slower times, life was as busy and hectic as it is today.

We are fortunate that Frith was a photographer of the people, dedicated to recording the minutiae of everyday life. For it is this sheer wealth of visual data, the painstaking chronicle of changes in dress, transport, street layouts, buildings, housing, engineering and landscape that captivates us so much today. His remarkable images offer us a powerful link with the past and with the lives of our ancestors.

Today's Technology

Computers have now made it possible for Frith's many thousands of images to be accessed almost instantly. In the Frith archive today, each photograph is carefully 'digitised' then stored on a CD Rom. Frith archivists can locate a single photograph amongst thousands within seconds. Views can be catalogued and sorted under a variety of categories of place and content to the immediate benefit of researchers.

Inexpensive reference prints can be created for them at the touch of a mouse button, and a wide range of books and other printed materials assembled and published for a wider, more general readership - in the next twelve months over a hundred Frith local history titles will be published! The day-to-day workings of the archive are very different from how they were in Francis Frith's time: imagine the herculean task of sorting through eleven tons of glass negatives as Frith had to do to locate a particular sequence of pictures! Yet

See Frith at www. frithbook.co.uk

the archive still prides itself on maintaining the same high standards of excellence laid down by Francis Frith, including the painstaking cataloguing and indexing of every view.

It is curious to reflect on how the internet now allows researchers in America and elsewhere greater instant access to the archive than Frith himself ever enjoyed. Many thousands of individual views can be called up on screen within seconds on one of the Frith internet sites, enabling people living continents away to revisit the streets of their ancestral home town, or view places in Britain where they have enjoyed holidays. Many overseas researchers welcome the chance to view special theme selections, such as transport, sports, costume and ancient monuments.

We are certain that Francis Frith would have heartily approved of these modern developments in imaging techniques, for he himself was always working at the very limits of Victorian photographic technology.

The Value of the Archive Today

Because of the benefits brought by the computer, Frith's images are increasingly studied by social historians, by researchers into genealogy and ancestory, by architects, town planners, and by teachers and schoolchildren involved in local history projects.

In addition, the archive offers every one of us an opportunity to examine the places where we and our families have lived and worked down the years. Highly successful in Frith's own era, the archive is now, a century and more on, entering a new phase of popularity.

The Past in Tune with the Future

Historians consider the Francis Frith Collection to be of prime national importance. It is the only archive of its kind remaining in private ownership and has been valued at a million pounds. However, this figure is now rapidly increasing as digital technology enables more and more people around the world to enjoy its benefits.

Francis Frith's archive is now housed in an historic timber barn in the beautiful village of Teffont in Wiltshire. Its founder would not recognize the archive office as it is today. In place of the many thousands of dusty boxes containing glass plate negatives and an all-pervading odour of photographic chemicals, there are now ranks of computer screens. He would be amazed to watch his images travelling round the world at unimaginable speeds through network and internet lines.

The archive's future is both bright and exciting. Francis Frith, with his unshakeable belief in making photographs available to the greatest number of people, would undoubtedly approve of what is being done today with his lifetime's work. His photographs, depicting our shared past, are now bringing pleasure and enlightenment to millions around the world a century and more after his death.

Middlesex - *An Introduction*

SURELY NO ENGLISH county has altered quite as much as Middlesex in recent times. It is almost as though the powers-that-be have attempted to squeeze Middlesex out of existence in a series of municipal changes over a century and a half. As long ago as 1888, Middlesex lost 50 square miles and two and a half million inhabitants to the County of London. The Greater London Council snatched a further nine of its local authorities in 1965, and several more were transferred to the Counties of Surrey and Hertfordshire in the same decade.

Yet Middlesex is one of England's most ancient and noble counties. Situated between the lands of the Saxons of Wessex and East Anglia, it acquired its name at least as early as 704 AD, when a charter described it as Middelseaxan - 'the land of the middle Saxons'. But Middlesex's long history goes back well before those troubled times. The Thames, the broadest and most beautiful of its rivers, was a highway from the time that mankind first occupied these islands: its waters penetrated the forests and swamps that made land passage arduous, if not impossible. By the Iron Age, land was already being cleared for farming, and settlements were starting to be established. The Romans used the Thames too; they established an administrative base called Londinium - London - and pushed mighty roads such as Watling Street and Akeman Street out across the countryside. Thus, this was already an important farming and trading area, supplying grain to fast-growing settlements, when the Saxons arrived.

Our second-smallest county had mighty London as its capital for centuries. However, the city merchants considered that London was the dominant half of the partnership, and that the countryside beyond was a kind of backyard - a place which produced agricultural goods and a location for accessible country houses. London even had the right to appoint Middlesex's Sheriff, and to control trade up the tidal reaches of the Thames as far as Staines. It could be argued that the modern use of Middlesex as a location for London's suburbia and overflow industry is simply a development of this ancient practice. But both London and Middlesex are really interdependent. Much of the city's water supply still comes from the great reservoirs of Middlesex.

The days when Westminster, Hampstead, Islington and Hammersmith were part of Middlesex are long gone; they were taken into Greater London. Yet some of the county's most important towns and best scenery remain. There is an active resistance movement amongst local residents - valiantly led by the Middlesex Society - to ensure that no more valuable ground is given and that the ancient traditions of this particular home county are maintained.

A first impression, certainly if we take the main routes into London, is that Middlesex has become totally urbanised, full of factories, housing estates and ribbon development. But that would be both a superficial and inaccurate view. Much of old Middlesex remains, as do most of the old buildings in the photographs that follow.

To get a good first view of this county, travel up the Thames by boat, from Westminster to Staines, perhaps, or walk the Thames Path, the long-distance trail that follows the river from mouth to source. This is Middlesex at its best, and probably oldest, for this is the original water highway that the Catevellauni, the Belgic tribe that settled here in the first century BC, would have known. Twickenham, Teddington and Hampton are still attractive riverside communities, for all their sprawl. The emphasis is now on pleasure boating on the Thames, and there are few more delightful sights than sailing dinghies racing along the river on regatta days. It is interesting to see from the Frith photographs how pleasure boats and trading vessels co-existed for so long on this same stretch of water and its connecting canals.

The joy of the Thames is Hampton Court Palace, delightful in its setting, and one of the leading historic attractions of England. Walking through this venerable old building or around its gardens or famous maze, it is easy to bring to mind those forceful personalities from Tudor history who resided here - Cardinal Wolsey, Henry VIII and Elizabeth I. They probably used the Thames to reach this great country house, in the way that some tourists still do; though the modern visitor can just enjoy the scenery, rather than having to wrestle with the cares of state. The palace was the

Tudor's 'place in the country'; the growth of villa residences nearby shows that workaday people have since emulated the monarchy in their desire to get out of town.

Two hundred years ago, William Cobbett, that most critical of commentators, described Middlesex as 'all ugly' - and this at a time when it must have been an idyllic rural paradise when compared to the Middlesex of today. Yet the modern visitor must admire places such as Pinner, with its country town atmosphere, and Harrow, with its old school, and a host of other towns and villages that would be assets to any other English county. All of this seems very defensive, as though some special case has to be made out for Middlesex. But that is not really so. It is more that we take Middlesex for granted, with the huge urban bulk of London on one side and more rural counties all around.

Middlesex scores very well in the culture stakes. Shakespeare is known to have acted at one country house here, and Lord Byron, John Keats, Alexander Pope, Oliver Goldsmith, John Milton, Virginia Woolf, Charles Dickens and Charles Lamb all have connections with the county and found inspiration during their times here. An entire British film industry thrived at Ealing and Shepperton for much of the 20th century, producing some of the classic movies of all time. Teddington and Ealing have connections with some of the best television programmes of recent decades, and there is a thriving theatrical scene. Many actors and writers have made their homes in Middlesex towns, and artists such as Kneller and Turner have worked here. The explorer with a bit of time to spare, and who is not put off by superficial impressions, can find as much to occupy his or her time in Middlesex as in any other county.

The Frith photographers caught Middlesex at a valuable time in its history, just before industry and its associated urban sprawl took over. In the photographs that follow we see the old settlements when they really were just country towns and villages. Those were halcyon days, when the few motorists could simply park at the side of the road with little fear of a parking ticket, and when walkers and cyclists had country lanes more or less to themselves. There is a fine selection of views of county churches, which remain fascinating places to visit despite some unfortunate Victorian restoration. Most contain the tombs of the great men and women who shaped Middlesex's destiny through the wider picture of English history.

The photographs show us the modern buildings as well, all telling the story of our recent social history; we can see market halls where farmers traded grain, town halls where local politicians sought to preserve the county's integrity, cinemas from the early days of silent films, and shopping streets - many boasting those delightful shop fronts that everyone enjoyed in the days before the deadening hand of the municipal planner was loosed upon urban England.

We are shown quieter scenes as well, including the relaxing country pub, the focus of many a modern community; the stroller on the canal towpath; sailing boats and punts on the Thames; and narrowboats making their way on their regular runs up and down the Grand Union Canal. Elsewhere, tents are pitched at the waterside, and bathers plunge into Middlesex's old water highways. The shoppers of several generations are just about everywhere, in what seems a gentler and less-hurried commercial age.

Just looking at this collection of photographs tells us as much about the social history of our time as the topography and history of this county. Yet many of the scenes illustrated by the Frith photographers can be sought out by the modern-day explorer of Middlesex, and found to be not really changed in the essentials. Middlesex is the most misunderstood and unappreciated of English counties. It deserves better!

▼ **Ashford, Rowlands Hill Almhouses 1895** 36019
Ashford, situated in the south-west corner of the county, takes its name
from an ancient river crossing, the Exeford of the Domesday Book. These
almshouses were provided for the relief of the elderly poor, and were
renowned for their high standard when they were built.

▼ **Ashford, The Cinema 1921** 70311
This impressive picture house shows how popular moving pictures had become in
the first decade after the Great War. Earlier film shows had taken place in theatres,
music halls, exhibitions and even circus tents. The silent film on offer when this
photograph was taken was 'Daredevil Jack', a feature about Jack Dempsey, the
fighter. Notice how the hoarding boasts the legend 'Living Pictures'.

▲ **Brentford
A County Town c1955**
B400017
In the days when
Middlesex encompassed
much of what is now
Greater London,
Brentford remained the
important county town,
though the title was more
or less ceremonial - real
administrative power lay
elsewhere. At one time
Brentford boasted a great
many coaching inns, for
the town was the first
stage for stagecoaches
leaving London on the
Great West Road to Bath
and Exeter.

◄ Cowley
The Lock c1955 C581002
A bare mile from the larger town of Uxbridge lies Cowley, set attractively in a setting of river and canals. Though increasingly suburbanised during the past century, there are some delightful waterside walks past the canal locks, such as this one.

◄ **Cowley, High Road c1960** C581008
Cowley, as is typical of the fast-growing towns of the 20th century, boasts all the facilities of a near-London satellite town, including this row of very functional shops - built to serve the growing community nearby.

◄ Cowley, Iver Lane c1955 C581005
In the parish churchyard at Cowley lies the body of William Dodd, novelist, religious author and social celebrity. This unfortunate writer attempted to secure preferment in the Church of England by bribery, and was made a social outcast when his crime was discovered. Dodd compounded his felony by trying to forge the name of the Earl of Chesterfield on a bond for £4200. Despite interventions by Dr Johnson, Dodd was hanged at Tyburn in 1777.

▼ Cranford, The Village c1965 C542010
As with so many towns to the west of London, Cranford lies on the old stagecoach route to the fashionable city of Bath. Cranford was surrounded by wild heathlands in coaching days, acquiring notoriety for the vast number of highwaymen who preyed on early travellers.

◄ Cranford, The Berkeley Arms Hotel c1965 C542011
This substantial hotel and public house takes its name from the Berkeley family, who lived nearby at Cranford House. Their great house was pulled down in the 1930s, and only a few tombs in the parish church are there to remind us of how powerful this local family once were.

Cranford, The Post Office c1965 C542005
Apart from the parish church, little remains of the Cranford that the Berkeleys would have known. The routes into the town have become built up with houses and bungalows, like so much of Middlesex. Some rural corners remain for anyone with time on their hands to explore.

Cranford, The Church of the Holy Angels c1965 C542003
The District Church of the Holy Angels began its existence in a steel hut. It had a hooter instead of bells to summon the faithful to prayer, and a dominant floodlight to illuminate the preacher of the day. The notice-board below the clock promotes the important Christmas services.

Ealing, Uxbridge Road c1901 E63501
Ealing had been a modest village in Middlesex with a population of
7000 at the beginning of Queen Victoria's reign. When Victoria
died in 1901 the population had increased to 47,000, thanks to
the urban sprawl of nearby London and the many people who
chose to settle in this attractive town upwind of the metropolis. The
advertising hoardings on the horse-drawn buses advertise both
Nestle's milk and Lipton's teas.

**Ealing
The Mall 1951** E63001
Ealing remains an
attractive place to live
and was, at the time this
photograph was taken,
a leading centre of the
British film industry. In
the distance is the spire
of Christ Church,
designed by Sir George
Gilbert Scott and
completed in 1852.

▼ **Ealing, The Town c1950** E63004
Ealing's proximity to London by public transport attracts many city workers, though the town has never succumbed to being merely a residential area for commuters. Many locals still work in and around Ealing, and the town has retained its excellent shopping centre.

▼ **Ealing, New Broadway c1965** E63064
A famous resident of Ealing was Sarah Trimmer, a friend of Dr Johnson, and writer of children's versions of the Scriptures. Sarah Trimmer was much loved by her contemporaries for her dedication to the education of the poor. She died in 1810, and lies buried in the parish church.

▲ **Edgware
The Station c1955**
E126027
This London Transport station at Edgware was designed by the notable architect Charles Holden; it opened in 1925. Edgware, once the first village beyond London, was a good location for such an important public transport depot.

◀ **Enfield
Church Street c1955**
E179039
There was probably a settlement at Enfield when the Roman legions marched along nearby Ermine Street, the important Roman highway that can still be seen adjacent to Enfield's High Street. Enfield remained a modest country town, clustered about what had once been a clearing in a great forest, well into the 20th century.

**Enfield
Church Street c1950**
E179007
Charles Lamb, the essayist, came to live in the country town of Enfield two centuries ago. Lamb and his sister Mary loved Enfield, and were a familiar sight as they took their constitutional walks along its streets and rural byways.

Enfield
The Market Square c1950 E179008
Much of early 19th-century literary society visited the Lambs at
Enfield, including the poets Wordsworth, Coleridge and Leigh Hunt,
and the essayist William Hazlitt. These celebrities would have seen
the Market Square still being used for agricultural purposes, though
the attractive octagonal Market House dates back only to
Edwardian times.

Enfield, St Mark's Road c1955 E179037
It was while staying at Enfield that Henry VIII's only legitimate male child became Edward VI on the death of his father. Edward later gifted the royal palace of Enfield to his favourite half-sister Elizabeth - later Queen Elizabeth I. The palace was demolished in the 18th century, and little remains of this once splendid building.

Enfield, The Swimming Pool c1955 E179025
Despite its closeness to London, Enfield has always been a self-sustaining community, with many municipally-backed leisure facilities such as this impressive swimming pool, which we see here being enjoyed by locals on a hot summer's day.

Enfield, The Town c1960 E179040
This busy mid 20th-century street scene shows a fine collection of shop fronts. This was about the last period in Enfield's history when the on-street parking of vehicles was quite so easy - note the complete absence of yellow lines.

◄ **Greenford**
The Broadway c1965
G242009
Greenford remained a village of modest proportions until the early years of the last century. Its original parish church dates back to at least the 15th century, though this was superseded as the town's major place of worship when a new church was built in 1939.

Enfield
London Road c1960
E179042
For many early travellers, Enfield was just the first stage in the long journey to the north of England. Many visitors thought Enfield such an attractive place to live that they chose to settle there.

▼ Greenford
The Cross-roads
c1965 G242006
Greenford lies at the very heart of the old administrative county of Middlesex, which originally included much of what is now Greater London. The town has remained a favourite place of residence for commuting city workers.

◄ Greenford
Greenford Road c1965
G242010
As the number of cars increased, many Greenford residents chose to use public transport when commuting into London. But for those who did not, one of the advantages of modern and expanding towns was that the shopping streets could be made wider to cope with the demands of the internal combustion engine.

**Hampton
The Bridge 1890**
27212
Many consider that the south-western corner of the county, alongside the Thames, is Middlesex at its loveliest. The Thames has always been important as a boating centre; for centuries it was used as a great water highway, along which many of the greatest figures of English history were transported.

◀ **Hampton**
Thames Street c1950
H369004
Hampton tends to be overlooked by visitors to the nearby Tudor palace. This is a great pity, for it remains a charming waterside town - though it is seldom now as quiet as in this photograph. Halfway up the street on the right we see the sign of Mr Constable, boatbuilder, and in the distance is the parish church of St Mary, designed by Lapidge in 1831.

◄ Hampton, The River
c1955 H369011

In recent times, the Thames has been used more for pleasure than business. Regular yachting regattas are held at Hampton, and many owners keep their boats nearby. Hampton lies about four hours of cruising time from the centre of London.

▼ Hampton, Street Scene
c1950 H369002

Hampton boasts a long history of famous residents. Sir Christopher Wren lived and worked here, designing St. Paul's and recreating London after the Great Fire of 1666. Richard Steele, the pioneer journalist, dodged his creditors at a house in Hampton, and the actor David Garrick spent his last years nearby.

◄ Hampton Wick, Kingston Eyot 1890
23542

Hampton Wick lies three miles east of Hampton, on the west bank of the River Thames facing Kingston across the river. Here, villa residences line the banks of the Thames - many with direct access to the water for those owners who possess a boat.

**Hampton Wick
Street Scene c1965**
H401003
Here we have a reminder of those quiet days on English roads when motorists could park wherever they liked, and when trolley-bus lines adorned many an urban street. Hampton Wick remains a place of delightful shops - a place to linger and browse.

**Hampton Court
The Palace c1950** H17007
King Henry VIII appropriated Hampton Court after the fall of Cardinal Wolsey, who had begun work on the great house as an imposing residence for himself. Henry and his succeeding children loved Hampton Court, and spent a great deal of time here. Every monarch until George III used Hampton Court as a royal palace. William and Mary engaged Wren to extend and improve the building. It remains a favourite day out for visitors from London and the Home Counties.

◄ Hampton Court
The River c1960 H17081

A boat awaits its passengers for the trip down-river to London. The Thames Passenger Service sign tells us that boats depart to Kingston and Richmond every half-hour. The fare is 2s 6d single to Kingston, and 3s 6d return, and to Richmond it is 4s single and 5s 6d return. To travel all the way downstream to Westminster it cost 6s 6d, with a return fare of 10s.

▼ Harefield
The Cross Roads
c1965 H428040

Harefield is situated at the north-western corner of Middlesex. Its charming medieval church is much visited by all who love fine ecclesiastical architecture. On one side of the broad green is the half-timbered King's Arms Inn, an attractive hostelry dating back to the 17th century.

◄ Harefield, Northwood
Road c1965 H428042

In Harefield Church is the elaborate tomb of Alice Spencer, Countess of Derby, who died in 1636. Lady Alice was a popular figure at the Elizabethan court, and the Queen spent three memorable days at her Harefield home - a visit enlivened by a production of 'Othello', in which Shakespeare himself probably acted. In old age Alice Spencer became a good friend to John Milton.

▼ **Harefield, The Canal c1965** H428034
By the time that this photograph was taken, the two hundred-year heyday of Britain's canal network had come to an end - though a few working boats remained. The canals of Middlesex have now acquired a new use as outlets for leisure boating, walks and nature study.

▼ **Harrow on the Hill, The Terrace 1906** 55685
Harrow on the Hill well deserves its name, for it is said that thirteen counties can be glimpsed from this Middlesex upland. Harrow School, one of the most prestigious in England, has provided Britain with several prime ministers, including Peel, Palmerston and Churchill.

▲ **Harrow on the Hill Bessborough Road 1906** 55683
Lord Byron, a schoolboy at Harrow, spent a great deal of time resting on the stone tomb of John Peachey in the churchyard, composing early verses and admiring the extensive view. His poem 'Spot of my Youth' muses 'Here might I sleep where all my hopes arose, Scene of my youth and couch of my repose'.

◀ **Harrow on the Hill
Moat Farm, Headstone
1906** 55688
This view of the countryside
near to Harrow reminds us
of the rural county that
Middlesex was until the
earlier years of the past
century. Perhaps this view is
not so very different from
the landscape that Byron
would have known.

Harrow
Station Road c1955 H429039
Harrow remains a favourite shopping centre for both local people
and the many visitors who come to view the famous school.
Harrow School occupied just one building until around 1800. Then
it began a rapid expansion, with the erection of new buildings and
the taking-over of existing properties.

Hendon, The Town Hall c1955 H397030
Hendon owes its rapid growth in the 20th century to the extension of the Northern Line of the underground, which made it an ideal outer London location for commuters. This imposing town hall was designed by the popular Victorian architect Watson; it opened in 1900.

Hendon, The Technical College c1965 H397029
Just along from the town hall is the old technical college building, an equally impressive structure. It was designed by H W Burchett and completed in 1937. The high ground on which this central part of the town is built gave Hendon its name, which derives from the Saxon and means 'high hill'.

**Hendon
Vivian Avenue c1965**
H397107
Hendon has long been associated with air transport, for the world's first airmail service began here in 1911 when messages were flown to Windsor to mark the Coronation of King George V. The Royal Air Force has used the nearby aerodrome for flying training and air displays for much of the last century.

**Hendon
The Broadway c1965**
H397149
Sir Stamford Raffles, the
founder of Singapore, is
buried at Hendon. A
self-educated man,
Raffles worked hard for
the welfare of the native
peoples of the Far East,
instigating education
programmes and
abolishing slavery. He
was only 44 when he
died.

◀ **Hendon
The Metropolitan
Police College c1965**
H397065
Hendon became the
training college for
would-be London police
officers in the last
century. It continues to
be the place where new
recruits are trained in
police procedure at the
present time.

Hendon, The Central Circus c1965 H397119

Hendon did not develop as a major shopping centre until well into the 20th century, when the rapid increase in the population made it necessary to provide better facilities for residents. Hendon's population in 1921 was only 16,000. In the next thirty years it had increased by another 130,000.

Hendon The Metropolitan Police College c1965

H397057

Heston, The Parish Church c1955 H251015

Heston, too, had early links with air travel; it was at one time the nearest airfield to central London. The parish church of St. Leonard's, seen here, is mostly a Victorian restoration - only the west tower and doorway have survived intact from the 15th century.

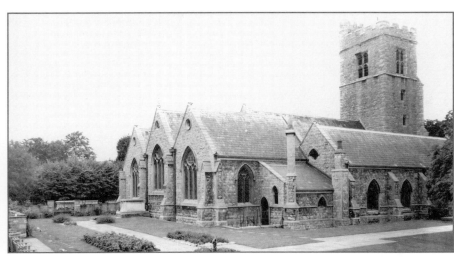

▼ Heston, Osterley Park c1965   H251028

Some of Osterley Park is Tudor, though most of the present building dates to around 1761 when Robert Adam was commissioned to decorate the house. The old manor had belonged to nearby Syon Abbey until the Dissolution, when Henry VIII seized it. Successive owners have included Elizabeth I, Sir Thomas Gresham and the Roundhead General William Waller. In more recent times the Earls of Jersey have held the estate. Osterley's garden of historic trees contains seedlings from many famous trees of past times: these include the Hatfield Oak, under which Elizabeth I learnt that she had become queen, a rose from the tomb of Omar Khayyam and a box tree from the battlefield at Waterloo.

▼ Hillingdon, The Circus and the Golden Lion c1950   H431007

A great deal of modern Hillingdon has become a satellite town for neighbouring Uxbridge. In the churchyard is the tomb of John Rich, the theatrical entrepreneur who unleashed John Gay's 'The Beggar's Opera' upon the world - to the good fortune of both men.

▲ Hillingdon
King's Parade
Long Lane c1950
H431008

◀ Hillingdon King's Parade c1950

H431001

Hillingdon, like so many towns in Middlesex, grew considerably during the last century. However, some green spaces remain to remind us of the days when Charles I retreated to the village here during the closing stages of the English Civil War.

Hillingdon, The Railway Station c1960 H431034
It was the rapid expansion of affordable public transport that led to the growth of Middlesex over the last hundred years. For the first time in London's history a large proportion of city workers could gain employment in the city's crowded streets and still be back in the Home Counties in time for tea.

Hounslow, Staines Road c1955 H162001
Beyond Hounslow, the Great West Road divided into the two coaching routes leading to Bath and Exeter. The long main street of the town gives a feeling that this was a community grown up around a great highway. Most of Hounslow's old coaching inns have now disappeared, or have been altered beyond recognition.

Hounslow, Street Scene c1955 H162006
Hounslow has changed a great deal since the heady days when several hundred stagecoaches a day passed along its great street. The once-notorious Hounslow Heath, the haunt of such famous highwaymen as Dick Turpin and Claude Duvall, has been urbanised and retains little of its old atmosphere.

Hounslow
Street Scene c1965 H162014
Much of modern Hounslow dates from the last century; it remains
a busy shopping centre. In the skies above are often seen jet
aircraft from the nearby Heathrow Airport - a form of transport that
would have been unimaginable to those early coach travellers.

Ickenham, St Giles's Church c1965 159001
Ickenham has retained a pleasant village atmosphere, despite some unfortunate modern building. The parish church dates back to the 14th century, with 16th-century additions from when the simple old building was enlarged.

Ickenham, The Pump c1965 159003
This good view of the village pump captures some of the feel of the old village of Ickenham. The road has been widened substantially since this communal water supply was in regular use.

**Ickenham
Swakeleys Road
c1965** I59019
A busy traffic junction
leads out from
Ickenham to the great
house of Swakeleys.
This photograph shows
some of the newer
buildings making up this
still-growing town.

Ickenham, Swakeleys House c1965 159013
Sir Edmund Wright, sometime Lord Mayor of London, built this lovely Jacobean house. A later owner, Sir Robert Vyner, notoriously cooked one of his deceased servants, displaying the corpse in an open coffin to visitors - a macabre spectacle that delighted Samuel Pepys who recorded the event in his diary.

Ickenham, Uxbridge Golf Club, The Club House c1965 159017
The huge growth in Middlesex's population has meant the creation of many golf courses on the green fields and heathlands of the county. A drink at the clubhouse is always a welcome attraction after a thoughtful game of golf.

Kenton
Kenton Road c1960 K151007
Just a century ago a great deal of lonely countryside
remained around Kenton, which lies on the road to
Harrow. The area is now urbanised; but an Edwardian
commentator remarked that it was quite possible to walk
Kenton's field paths and never see a soul.

◀ **Kingsbury
The Broadway
and Station Parade
c1950** K142013
Kingsbury's heavy clay
soil resisted early
attempts at mass
house-building, and it
remained a village well
into the 20th century.
Its surroundings
remained one of the
'green lungs' of outer
London until more
recently. The old
Gaumont cinema can
be see on the left-hand
side of the road.

Kingsbury, The Circle ▶
c1955 K142023
The heathlands around
modern-day Kingsbury
were once hunted over
by Stone Age dwellers.
Roman legions marched
this way and, as the Old
English name suggests,
this village was
important in Anglo-
Saxon times.

**◄ Kingsbury
Kingsbury Road
c1955** K142020
An Edwardian
guidebook describes
this area as being so
rural that 'blackberries
can grow ripe here
within sound of the
Metropolitan Railway
and the plainest hint of
London's close
neighbourhood is a
crop of notices to
trespassers'. The
trespass notices have
gone, but blackberries
may still be found.

Kingsbury ▶
Kingsbury Road
c1955 K142017
Below the telephone
kiosk are the offices of
Carter, Paterson and
Pickfords, the
celebrated removal and
carrier firm. Kingsbury
was once an important
horse-breeding centre;
most of London would
turn out for the
Kingsbury Races - once
an important occasion
in the sporting calendar.

**◄ Kingsbury
Kingsbury Road
c1955** K142016

Kingsbury, The Parish Church c1960 K142019
Kingsbury can boast of three distinctive churches. This is Butterfield's late Victorian edifice with its unusual polygonal turret; a smaller pre-Conquest building stands not far away, next to its modern replacement - an early Victorian church transported brick by brick from central London in 1933.

Kingsbury, The Swimming Pool c1965 K142048
This impressively large swimming pool was constructed for the benefit of the increasing population in this part of Middlesex. It was a welcome place for a dip on a hot day.

Laleham
The Church 1890 27264
Laleham's charming parish church has a tower dating back
to 1732; it has been altered somewhat since this photograph
was taken. In its churchyard is the grave of the Victorian
poet Matthew Arnold, with an epitaph which reads 'Awake,
thou Lute and Harp - I will awake right early'.

Laleham
The Village 1906
58005
Laleham was a tiny village when Dr Thomas Arnold, soon to be the formidable headmaster of Rugby School, came to live here in Regency times. His son Matthew, the poet, was born in Laleham in 1822, and spent the early years of his life here. Arnold's poetry and scholarship - he became Professor of Poetry at Oxford University at the very young age of 35 - was hugely influential. Matthew Arnold died in Liverpool in 1882, but was brought back to his birthplace for burial.

Laleham, The River 1934 86335
Old Laleham stands back from the reaches of the Thames, and the early boating fraternity used to enjoy catching glimpses of it from the water. William Morris recorded an impression of 'enormous willows and queer suggestions of old houses on the banks'.

Laleham The River 1934 86332
A summer day, a tent on the banks of the Thames, and the opportunity for a bathe in the river. This was an idyllic time in a quieter less-crowded Middlesex in those halcyon days before World War Two.

Perivale, Bilton Road c1965 P304019

Inhabitants of medieval London were fed from the wheatfields of Perivale, though there are fewer green areas in the locality these days. The huge Hoover factory - the manufacturing place of millions of vacuum cleaners - dominated more recent Perivale.

Perivale, The Canal c1965 P304012
This old canal is quiet and empty in the latter half of the 20th century, its busiest times as a trade highway only a distant memory. Its towpath remains a delightful place for an evening stroll.

Pinner, The Memorial Gardens c1955 P296028
A famous resident of Pinner was Horatia Ward, the illegitimate daughter of Admiral Lord Nelson and Lady Hamilton. A child when her father was killed at Trafalgar, Horatia married Philip Ward, the vicar of Tenterden, and then spent her long widowhood at Pinner. This country town grew thanks to the passage of the Metropolitan Railway through the district, which attracted commuting residents. Pinner remains one of the most attractive towns in Middlesex.

◀ Pinner, The Old Oak Tea Rooms c1955
P296020
Pinner boasts an impressive number of lovely old buildings, some of which have been transformed into tea and antique shops. It would be high on the list of most people's favourite London suburbs.

▼ Hatch End, The Broadway c1965   H404021
At one end of Pinner is the overspill community of Hatch End. Notice the old-style W H Smith shop front on the street corner; a common sight in most towns until a few decades ago.

**Shepperton
The Lock 1890** 23580
Many devotees of
boating consider that
the River Thames is
at its best around
Shepperton, particularly
when a regatta is being
held, with boats
crowding the river and
excited spectators lining
the banks. Not far from
the river are the famous
Shepperton Film
Studios, where many
a classic British movie
has been made.

Shepperton, A Backwater and the Church 1890 23584
Shepperton's church can be glimpsed from the Thames, but it is not often visited by those afloat. Built of flint rubble, this church replaced an earlier building that was submerged by the river. In the cemetery not far away lies Thomas Love Peacock, the Victorian writer of colourful novels, who lived at Lower Halliford.

Southall, The Manor House 1965 S616001
Now very much a part of north London, Southall boasts this attractive manor house, much used as the headquarters of a municipal department in recent years. The house dates back to at least 1587, though many builders have toyed with the original design in the intervening centuries.

Staines
Children by the River 1890 23601X
Two girls play with a hoop on the banks of the Thames,
not far from Staines. Historically, Staines marked the end
of the jurisdiction of the City of London over the river.
The Lord Mayor of London and Corporation would make
regular visits to Staines to assert their authority.

Staines, High Street 1895 35980
Staines was very much an agricultural area when this photograph was taken towards the end of Queen Victoria's reign; the shop fronts tell us a great deal about the commercial aspects of Victorian society. Watson's toys and fancy goods shop is also a registry office for servants - a way of putting servants in touch with potential employers. Further down the road are Johnson and Smith's Staines Ironworks; such local foundries were not uncommon in larger towns at this period. A little further, behind the stagecoach, are the Corn Stores, not just a supply outlet but a meeting place for local farmers. In the far distance are Morford and Goodman, furnishers.

**Staines
Clarence Street 1895**
35985
Staines may have got its name from the stone-paved remains of a branch of the Roman road of Akeman Street, that once ran to the important Roman station of Ad Pontes nearby, or perhaps from a Roman milestone that once stood here. Some have said that the name comes from the 'London Stone' or 'Staines Stone' which marked the jurisdiction of the city over the Thames at this point. Clarence Street dates probably from the time of the Georgian expansion of the town.

Staines, High Street 1907 57995
Staines, like so many Middlesex towns, stands on one of the principal coaching routes out of London - the Exeter Road. Most of the old coaching inns, of which there were many, have now disappeared. The Angel probably gets its name from the biblical Annunciation. By the time this photograph was taken, the great age of coaching was but a memory, ended by the construction of the railway. The Angel clearly sought a new clientele - hence the addition of 'Commercial' to its name.

**Staines
High Street 1907**
57997
Sir Walter Raleigh was
found guilty of treason
in the old Market House
at Staines, which has
since been demolished.
A plague had prevented
the Court from holding
the trial in London. A
short distance from
Staines is the site of an
earlier and very
important event in
English history,
Runnymede: here
Magna Carta was signed
by King John in 1215.

Staines
Bell Weir Lock 1907 58000
Boating on the Thames was a very popular recreation during the
long 'Edwardian afternoon'. In a short voyage, the excursionist
could land on either the Middlesex or Surrey banks of the Thames,
or go upstream to nearby Buckinghamshire.

Staines, Boating 1907 57989X
Staines's High Street leads down towards this bridge over the Thames. The three-arched structure was designed by George Rennie and opened by King William IV in the 1830s. Earlier attempts to build a long-lasting bridge over the river had not always met with success.

Stanwell, The Church 1895 36025
Stanwell lies on the northern side of the Staines reservoirs, and is now under the flight path of Heathrow Airport. However, it still manages to retain much of its village atmosphere. Its church is at least 13th-century in origin, though the larger part is later medieval. One feature is the tomb of Lord Knyvett, the official who discovered Guy Fawkes at work in the cellar under the Houses of Parliament.

Stanwell
The Post Office c1950 S588007
It was Lord Knyvett who left money in his will to endow a school in Stanwell. This gesture was probably meant as a memorial to Mary Stuart, sister of Charles I, who died in 1607 whilst under Knyvett's guardianship.

Stanwell, The River c1965 S588040
Here we see landing wharves on the Thames, a reminder of how important trade was to the river even as far
upstream as Stanwell. On Ridley's Wharf is the warehouse of Morgan and Son, timber importers.

Stanwell, The Rising Sun c1965 S588009
Children bathe in a brook on a hot day in Stanwell. Perhaps their parents are seeking a different kind
of refreshment in the nearby Rising Sun public house.

Sunbury
The Magpie Hotel
1890 23560
Sunbury is a Thameside
village, shared between
Middlesex and Surrey; it
expanded considerably
during the last century.
Kempton Park, now a
venue for horse-racing,
was once a royal
residence.

Sunbury, The Lock 1890 23563
Sunbury became a fashionable place to reside during the 17th century, and there are a number of fine houses in the town. The river scenery, with white water weirs and broad curving stretches of the Thames, is a delight.

Sunbury, The Church from the Bridge 1890 23565
St Mary's church is a mostly Victorian reconstruction, though parts are early Georgian. It was under a churchyard yew at Sunbury that Dickens sets the scene where Bill Sikes and Oliver rest before the burglary in 'Oliver Twist'.

Sunbury
Thames Street c1955 S248007
This scene reminds us of how quiet the roads of Middlesex could be even half a century ago. This photograph features one of Sunbury's public houses, the Flower Pot.

Sunbury, Street Scene c1955 S248028
This photograph shows another tranquil street scene from the 1950s, when traffic had not reached the levels it has now, clogging the roads and lanes of London's outer towns and villages. On the left is the Courage public house, the White Horse.

Teddington, The Weir 1890 23539
The Thames is tidal as far as Teddington; many Londoners are fond of the sight of the water tumbling over the famous weir. Nearby is the biggest lock on the river. It is still a busy water passage, with a great many pleasure craft passing through each day.

Teddington
The Lock and the Rollers 1899 43054
Just over a hundred years ago, the Thames and its network
of canals were used as much for transporting goods as for
pleasure boating. Here we can see a number of narrow
boats waiting to use the famous lock.

**Teddington
The Bridge 1899**
43050
A number of working
boats and pleasure craft
are moored below
Teddington Bridge. The
sign on the half-hidden
building reads 'Albion
Boat House, Punt and
Boat Builder,
Showrooms'.

▼ **Teddington, The Lock c1960** T19008
Teddington's population grew from around 1,000 inhabitants in mid-Victorian times to over 25,000 just a century later. Many found it a pleasant town to live in, not too far from London. One famous resident was R D Blackmore, the author of 'Lorna Doone' and 'Christowell', who worked here as a market gardener, writing his novels in his spare time.

▼ **Teddington, High Street c1960** T19024
One much-loved inhabitant was the actress Peg Woffington, who died here at the age of 39. Peg Woffington created the role of Polly Peachum in Gay's 'The Beggars' Opera', and became the toast of London society in the early 18th century. Tradition says that she gave away much of her fortune to the poor people of Teddington - she may have endowed the local almshouses.

▲ **Teddington Broad Street c1955**
T19020
An earlier resident was John Walter, who died in 1812 and lies buried in the parish church. Walter was a coal merchant who diversified into printing and then journalism; he founded the 'Times' newspaper in the 1780s.

◄ **Twickenham From the Island Boat House 1890** 23534
In the last two hundred years this once-modest village has grown into a considerable town, lining miles of the river with streets and villas. This scene shows the working Victorian river that Charles Dickens would have known when he worked here on 'Oliver Twist' some years earlier.

**Twickenham
The Island 1890**

23535

Racing boats are drawn up outside the establishment of Mr C Shore - an appropriate name that was much punned upon by his contemporaries. The sign on his office reads 'C Shore, Waterman, Boats Built, Repaired and Let'.

**◄ Twickenham
The Church 1899**
43059
St Mary's Church dates
from the 15th century,
though much of the
present building is a
reconstruction by John
James, after the original
church fell down in
1713. The Thames has
occasionally flooded the
church; a mark on the
building shows how high
the waters have reached.

Twickenham
The Queen's Head Inn 1890
23536A

Most visitors hold that the narrow streets around the church are the most charming part of Twickenham. The street pattern that the poet Alexander Pope would have known is there to be seen, though Pope's original villa - some distance away - has been replaced by a more modern building.

Twickenham
York House 1899   43543

Charles II gave the original York House to the Earl of Clarendon, who generously gave his home to his son-in-law James II. The last two Stuart queens of England, Mary and Anne, were born here. The present house dates from around 1700.

Twickenham
Street Scene c1955
T91022

A number of other writers since Pope have found Twickenham an inspiring place to work. Charles Dickens wrote parts of 'Oliver Twist' at Ailsa Park Villas, and Dickens's literary hero Henry Fielding wrote 'Tom Jones' - one of the earliest of English novels - in a long-vanished house in Back Lane.

Twickenham
The Sports Ground c1960 T91046
Twickenham has enjoyed a long association with the British game
of rugby football. As early as 1867, the young men of Wellesley
House Academy were playing matches against the senior
Richmond Rugby Football Club. By the early 1870s, a club had
been formed in Twickenham; by the turn of the next century, it was
playing most of Britain's senior clubs. Twickenham remains one of
the most important venues for rugby football.

Twickenham
Traffic c1960 T91038

It was in a Twickenham drawing room that George IV, when Prince of Wales, secretly married his mistress Maria Fitzherbert. This action was contrary to the Royal Marriages Act, for George was under 25 and Maria was a Roman Catholic. Although they lived as a couple afterwards, neither Parliament nor the Royal Family recognised their union. George subsequently married Caroline of Brunswick, though on their separation he lived once again with Maria. Maria Fitzherbert, an uncrowned Queen of England, died at Brighton in 1837.

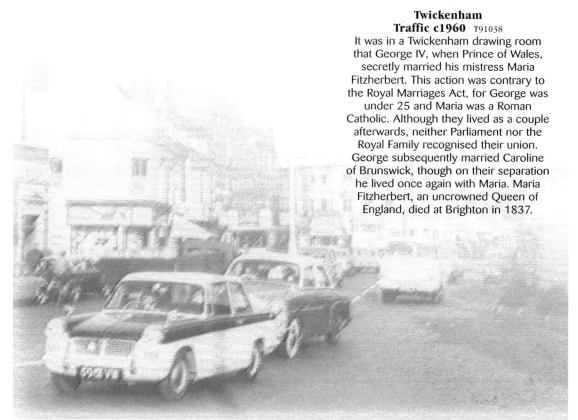

**Twickenham
A Street Corner
c1960** T91039

▼ **Uxbridge, The Grand Union Canal c1955** U52006
There is some delightful waterside scenery around Uxbridge, for it is situated not far from the banks of the rivers Fray and Colne. The Grand Union Canal, which runs from London to the Midlands, was opened for trade in 1770. These days its narrowboats are more likely to belong to holidaymakers than to the commercial operators seen here at work.

▼ **Uxbridge, The Canal c1955** U52030
A peaceful journey by canal is a wonderful way to see the county of Middlesex. Much of it is greener than people imagine. The slow pace of the narrowboat or a ramble along the towpath is just the right speed to appreciate its scenery and history.

▲ **Uxbridge
The Old Market Hall
c1950** U52023
Uxbridge's impressive Market Hall was built in 1789, though its frontage and appearance has altered somewhat since then. The ground floor was once open-plan, and was used for the buying and selling of corn. Grain was stored on the upper floor, which also housed a small school.

◀ **Uxbridge, High Street Looking East c1950**
U52015
In 1645, King Charles I and representatives of Parliament came together at Uxbridge to try and seek a negotiated end to the English Civil War. The King's stubbornness meant that nothing was achieved, and a final peace was to be years away. Charles was executed in 1649. All that remains of the Old Treaty House has been incorporated into the present Crown Hotel.

◄ **Uxbridge**
St Margaret's Church
c1965 U52033
Neighbouring Hillingdon was once a more important village than Uxbridge, and was home to the parish church. St. Margaret's began its existence as a chapel-of-ease, built so that the faithful need not go to the mother church for their acts of worship. Uxbridge increased in size during medieval times, and became a parish in its own right.

◀ Uxbridge
Windsor Street c1965
U52036
Windsor Street leads up to Uxbridge's parish church; it boasts a wonderful array of lovely old buildings, some of them pre-Georgian. How wonderful to be able to leave unattended bicycles propped up unlocked at the side of the road!

▼ West Drayton, The River c1965
W578017
The River Colne would have been a familiar sight to the Paget family, who lived at West Drayton's great manor house. William Paget was Secretary of State to Henry VIII, but fell from grace by taking the part of Protector Somerset during young King Edward's reign. Paget survived imprisonment in the Tower of London, but his misalliance cost him dear in both land and money. Paget's old home was demolished in 1750.

◀ West Drayton
Station Road c1965
W578002
Away from the heart of the old village, Station Road is relatively modern; there are few old buildings along its broad route. Notice the service road on the right, a largely post-war concept, designed to ease deliveries and parking.

Whitton, High Street c1965 W481007
Whitton is now just a part of sprawling Twickenham, though people have lived here since Saxon times. Its church, built only in 1862, looks medieval; some of its fittings were brought from older ecclesiastical buildings.

Whitton, The Military School of Music c1965 W481002
Kneller Hall, the famous home of military music, was originally built by the artist Kneller in the early 1700s. Little remains of that house. What we see today is George Mair's reconstruction of 1848. It remains a gracious building in a county of exquisite architecture.

Index

Frith Book Co Titles

www.frithbook.co.uk

The Frith Book Company publishes over 100 new titles each year. A selection of those currently available are listed below. For latest catalogue please contact Frith Book Co.

Town Books 96pp, 100 photos. County and Themed Books 128pp, 150 photos (unless specified). All titles hardback laminated case and jacket except those indicated pb (paperback)

Around Aylesbury (pb)	1-85937-227-9	£9.99	Down the Thames	1-85937-121-3	£14.99
Around Bakewell	1-85937-113-2	£12.99	Around Dublin	1-85937-058-6	£12.99
Around Barnstaple	1-85937-084-5	£12.99	Around Dublin (pb)	1-85937-231-7	£9.99
Around Bath	1-85937-097-7	£12.99	East Anglia (pb)	1-85937-265-1	£9.99
Berkshire (pb)	1-85937-191-4	£9.99	East London	1-85937-080-2	£14.99
Around Blackpool	1-85937-049-7	£12.99	East Sussex	1-85937-130-2	£14.99
Around Bognor Regis	1-85937-055-1	£12.99	Around Eastbourne	1-85937-061-6	£12.99
Around Bournemouth	1-85937-067-5	£12.99	Edinburgh (pb)	1-85937-193-0	£8.99
Around Bradford (pb)	1-85937-204-x	£9.99	English Castles	1-85937-078-0	£14.99
Brighton (pb)	1-85937-192-2	£8.99	English Country Houses	1-85937-161-2	£17.99
British Life A Century Ago	1-85937-103-5	£17.99	Around Exeter	1-85937-126-4	£12.99
British Life A Century Ago (pb)	1-85937-213-9	£9.99	Exmoor	1-85937-132-9	£14.99
Buckinghamshire (pb)	1-85937-200-7	£9.99	Around Falmouth	1-85937-066-7	£12.99
Camberley (pb)	1-85937-222-8	£9.99	Folkestone	1-85937-124-8	£9.99
Around Cambridge	1-85937-092-6	£12.99	Gloucestershire	1-85937-102-7	£14.99
Cambridgeshire	1-85937-086-1	£14.99	Around Great Yarmouth	1-85937-085-3	£12.99
Canals and Waterways	1-85937-129-9	£17.99	Greater Manchester (pb)	1-85937-266-x	£9.99
Cardiff (pb)	1-85937-093-4	£9.99	Around Guildford	1-85937-117-5	£12.99
Carmarthenshire	1-85937-216-3	£14.99	Around Harrogate	1-85937-112-4	£12.99
Cheltenham (pb)	1-85937-095-0	£9.99	Hastings & Bexhill (pb)	1-85937-131-0	£9.99
Around Chester	1-85937-090-x	£12.99	Helston (pb)	1-85937-214-7	£9.99
Around Chichester	1-85937-089-6	£12.99	Herefordshire	1-85937-174-4	£14.99
Around Chichester (pb)	1-85937-228-7	£9.99	Around Horsham	1-85937-127-2	£12.99
Churches of Berkshire	1-85937-170-1	£17.99	Humberside	1-85937-215-5	£14.99
Churches of Dorset	1-85937-172-8	£17.99	Around Ipswich	1-85937-133-7	£12.99
Colchester (pb)	1-85937-188-4	£8.99	Ireland (pb)	1-85937-181-7	£9.99
Cornish Coast	1-85937-163-9	£14.99	Isle of Man	1-85937-065-9	£14.99
Cornwall	1-85937-054-3	£14.99	Isle of Wight	1-85937-114-0	£14.99
Cornwall (pb)	1-85937-229-5	£9.99	Kent (pb)	1-85937-189-2	£9.99
Cotswolds (pb)	1-85937-230-9	£9.99	Kent Living Memories	1-85937-125-6	£14.99
County Durham	1-85937-123-x	£14.99	Lancaster, Morecambe & Heysham (pb)		
Cumbria	1-85937-101-9	£14.99		1-85937-233-3	£9.99
Dartmoor	1-85937-145-0	£14.99	Leeds (pb)	1-85937-202-3	£9.99
Derbyshire (pb)	1-85937-196-5	£9.99	Around Leicester	1-85937-073-x	£12.99
Devon	1-85937-052-7	£14.99	Leicestershire (pb)	1-85937-185-x	£9.99
Dorset	1-85937-075-6	£14.99	Around Lincoln	1-85937-111-6	£12.99
Dorset Coast	1-85937-062-4	£14.99	Lincolnshire	1-85937-135-3	£14.99
Dorset Living Memories	1-85937-210-4	£14.99	London (pb)	1-85937-183-3	£9.99
Down the Severn	1-85937-118-3	£14.99	Ludlow (pb)	1-85937-176-0	£9.99

Available from your local bookshop or from the publisher

Frith Book Co Titles (continued)

Around Maidstone	1-85937-056-x	£12.99	South Devon Coast	1-85937-107-8	£14.99
Manchester (pb)	1-85937-198-1	£9.99	South Devon Living Memories	1-85937-168-x	£14.99
Peterborough (pb)	1-85937-219-8	£9.99	Staffordshire (96pp)	1-85937-047-0	£12.99
Piers	1-85937-237-6	£17.99	Stone Circles & Ancient Monuments		
New Forest	1-85937-128-0	£14.99		1-85937-143-4	£17.99
Around Newark	1-85937-105-1	£12.99	Around Stratford upon Avon	1-85937-098-5	£12.99
Around Newquay	1-85937-140-x	£12.99	Suffolk (pb)	1-85937-221-x	£9.99
Norfolk (pb)	1-85937-195-7	£9.99	Surrey (pb)	1-85937-240-6	£9.99
North Devon Coast	1-85937-146-9	£14.99	Sussex (pb)	1-85937-184-1	£9.99
North Yorks	1-85937-236-8	£9.99	Swansea (pb)	1-85937-167-1	£9.99
Norwich (pb)	1-85937-194-9	£8.99	Tees Valley & Cleveland	1-85937-211-2	£14.99
Around Nottingham	1-85937-060-8	£12.99	Thanet (pb)	1-85937-116-7	£9.99
Nottinghamshire (pb)	1-85937-187-6	£9.99	Tiverton (pb)	1-85937-178-7	£9.99
Around Oxford	1-85937-096-9	£12.99	Around Torbay	1-85937-063-2	£12.99
Peak District	1-85937-100-0	£14.99	Around Truro	1-85937-147-7	£12.99
Around Penzance	1-85937-069-1	£12.99	Victorian & Edwardian Kent	1-85937-149-3	£14.99
Around Plymouth	1-85937-119-1	£12.99	Victorian & Edwardian Maritime Album		
Norfolk Living Memories	1-85937-217-1	£14.99		1-85937-144-2	£17.99
North Yorks (pb)	1-85937-236-8	£9.99	Victorian and Edwardian Sussex	1-85937-157-4	£14.99
Preston (pb)	1-85937-212-0	£9.99	Victorian & Edwardian Yorkshire	1-85937-154-x	£14.99
Reading (pb)	1-85937-238-4	£9.99	Victorian Seaside	1-85937-159-0	£17.99
Salisbury (pb)	1-85937-239-2	£9.99	Warwickshire (pb)	1-85937-203-1	£9.99
Around St Ives	1-85937-068-3	£12.99	West Midlands	1-85937-109-4	£14.99
Around Scarborough	1-85937-104-3	£12.99	West Sussex	1-85937-148-5	£14.99
Scotland (pb)	1-85937-182-5	£9.99	West Yorkshire (pb)	1-85937-201-5	£9.99
Around Sevenoaks and Tonbridge	1-85937-057-8	£12.99	Weymouth (pb)	1-85937-209-0	£9.99
Somerset	1-85937-153-1	£14.99	Wiltshire Living Memories	1-85937-245-7	£14.99
South Hams	1-85937-220-1	£14.99	Around Winchester	1-85937-139-6	£12.99
Around Southampton	1-85937-088-8	£12.99	Windmills & Watermills	1-85937-242-2	£17.99
Around Southport	1-85937-106-x	£12.99	Worcestershire	1-85937-152-3	£14.99
Around Shrewsbury	1-85937-110-8	£12.99	York (pb)	1-85937-199-x	£9.99
Shropshire	1-85937-083-7	£14.99	Yorkshire Living Memories	1-85937-166-3	£14.99

Frith Book Co titles available 2001

Around Bedford (pb)	1-85937-205-8	£9.99	Lake District (pb)	1-85937-275-9	£9.99
Around Brighton (pb)	1-85937-192-2	£9.99	Liverpool and Merseyside (pb)	1-85937-234-1	£9.99
Buckinghamshire (pb)	1-85937-200-7	£9.99	Around Luton (pb)	1-85937-235-x	£9.99
Cheshire (pb)	1-85937-271-6	£9.99	Northumberland and Tyne & Wear (pb)		
Dorset (pb)	1-85937-269-4	£9.99		1-85937-281-3	£9.99
Devon (pb)	1-85937-297-x	£9.99	Peak District (pb)	1-85937-280-5	£9.99
Down the Thames (pb)	1-85937-278-3	£9.99	Surrey (pb)	1-85937-081-0	£9.99
Heart of Lancashire (pb)	1-85937-197-3	£9.99	Sussex (pb)	1-85937-184-1	£9.99
Hereford (pb)	1-85937-175-2	£9.99			

See Frith books on the internet www.frithbook.co.uk

FRITH PRODUCTS & SERVICES

Francis Frith would doubtless be pleased to know that the pioneering publishing venture he started in 1860 still continues today. A hundred and forty years later, The Francis Frith Collection continues in the same innovative tradition and is now one of the foremost publishers of vintage photographs in the world. Some of the current activities include:

Interior Decoration

Today Frith's photographs can be seen framed and as giant wall murals in thousands of pubs, restaurants, hotels, banks, retail stores and other public buildings throughout the country. In every case they enhance the unique local atmosphere of the places they depict and provide reminders of gentler days in an increasingly busy and frenetic world.

Product Promotions

Frith products are used by many major companies to promote the sales of their own products or to reinforce their own history and heritage. Frith promotions have been used by Hovis bread, Courage beers, Scots Porage Oats, Colman's mustard, Cadbury's foods, Mellow Birds coffee, Dunhill pipe tobacco, Guinness, and Bulmer's Cider.

Genealogy and Family History

As the interest in family history and roots grows world-wide, more and more people are turning to Frith's photographs of Great Britain for images of the towns, villages and streets where their ancestors lived; and, of course, photographs of the churches and chapels where their ancestors were christened, married and buried are an essential part of every genealogy tree and family album.

Frith Products

All Frith photographs are available Framed or just as Mounted Prints and Posters (size 23 x 16 inches). These may be ordered from the address below. From time to time other products - Address Books, Calendars, Table Mats, etc - are available.

The Internet

Already twenty thousand Frith photographs can be viewed and purchased on the internet. By the end of the year 2000 some 60,000 Frith photographs will be available on the internet. The number of sites is constantly expanding, each focussing on different products and services from the Collection.
The main Frith sites are listed below.
www.francisfrith.co.uk
www.frithbook.co.uk

See the complete list of Frith Books at:
www.frithbook.co.uk
This web site is regularly updated with the latest list of publications from the Frith Book Company. If you wish to buy books relating to another part of the country that your local bookshop does not stock, you may purchase on-line.

For further information, trade, or author enquiries please contact us at the address below:
The Francis Frith Collection, Frith's Barn, Teffont, Salisbury, Wiltshire, England SP3 5QP.
Tel: +44 (0)1722 716 376 Fax: +44 (0)1722 716 881   Email: sales@francisfrith.co.uk

See Frith books on the internet www.frithbook.co.uk

TO RECEIVE YOUR FREE MOUNTED PRINT

Mounted Print
Overall size 14 x 11 inches

Cut out this Voucher and return it with your remittance for £1.50 to cover postage and handling, to UK addresses. For overseas addresses please include £4.00 post and handling. Choose any photograph included in this book. Your SEPIA print will be A4 in size, and mounted in a cream mount with burgundy rule lines, overall size 14 x 11 inches.

Order additional Mounted Prints at HALF PRICE (only £7.49 each*)

If there are further pictures you would like to order, possibly as gifts for friends and family, purchase them at half price (no additional postage and handling required).

Have your Mounted Prints framed*

For an additional £14.95 per print you can have your chosen Mounted Print framed in an elegant polished wood and gilt moulding, overall size 16 x 13 inches (no additional postage and handling required).

---

* IMPORTANT!
These special prices are only available if ordered using the original voucher on this page (no copies permitted) and at the same time as your free Mounted Print, for delivery to the same address

---

Frith Collectors' Guild

From time to time we publish a magazine of news and stories about Frith photographs and further special offers of Frith products. If you would like 12 months FREE membership, please return this form.

Send completed forms to:
The Francis Frith Collection, Frith's Barn, Teffont, Salisbury, Wiltshire SP3 5QP

Voucher for **FREE** and Reduced Price Frith Prints

Picture no.	Page number	Qty	Mounted @ £7.49	Framed + £14.95	Total Cost
		1	**Free of charge***	£	£
			£7.49	£	£
			£7.49	£	£
			£7.49	£	£
			£7.49	£	£
			£7.49	£	£

Please allow 28 days for delivery   *** Post & handling**   **£1.50**

Book Title . . . .   **Total Order Cost**   **£**

Please do not photocopy this voucher. Only the original is valid, so please cut it out and return it to us.

I enclose a cheque / postal order for £ . . . .
made payable to 'The Francis Frith Collection'
OR please debit my Mastercard / Visa / Switch / Amex card
(credit cards please on all overseas orders)

Number . . . .

Issue No (Switch only) . . . . Valid from (Amex/Switch) . . . .

Expires . . . .   Signature . . . .

Name Mr/Mrs/Ms . . . .

Address . . . .

. . . .

. . . . Postcode . . . .

Daytime Tel No . . . .   Valid to 31/12/02

The Francis Frith Collectors' Guild

Please enrol me as a member for 12 months free of charge.

Name Mr/Mrs/Ms . . . .

Address . . . .

. . . .

. . . . Postcode . . . .

Free Print - see overleaf